Lottie Deno

Gambling Queen of Hearts

Lottie Deno

Gambling Queen of Hearts

Cynthia Rose

Clear Light Publishers
Santa Fe, New Mexico

Clear Light Publishers
823 Don Diego
Santa Fe, New Mexico 87501

Library of Congress Cataloging in Publication Data
Rose, Cynthia.

　　Lottie Deno : gambling queen of hearts / Cynthia Rose
　　　　p. cm.
　　ISBN 0-940666-38-3:
　　$12.95
　　　　1. Deno, Lottie. 2. Gamblers—West (U.S.)—Biography.
　　3. Philanthropists—West (U.S.)—Biography.
　　4. Women—West (U.S.)—Biography. I. Title.
　　HV6721.W38R67   1993
　　795' .092—dc20   93-5335
　　[B]   CIP

First Edition
10 9 8 7 6 5 4 3 2 1

Designed by Irving Warhaftig.
Printed in U.S.A.
Baker Johnson, Dexter, Michigan

To the city of Deming, New Mexico,
and to the memory of
Frank and Lottie Thurmond

Introduction

The literature on the American West includes monumental works on such notables as Wyatt Earp, Doc Holliday, Billy the Kid, Annie Oakley, and Calamity Jane. These characters and their exploits in the wild days of western expansion and settlement have captured our imagination; it is hard to believe that any individuals have been overlooked whose lives and adventures could be as exciting. Yet occasionally new information comes to light about old-timers whose lives bear comparison with the traditional legendary figures of the Old West.

In southern New Mexico, one small town, seldom mentioned in the chronicles, carries on daily with its regular routine. Travelers pass by the town of Deming, New Mexico, on their way to other places. They rarely stop, unless for food, gas, or lodging. Few would imagine that this little town was once a hub of activity, filled with roughnecks, railroad men, and miners, or that two of the West's most exciting characters made it their final home.

Frank and Charlotte Thurmond settled in Deming in 1882. Who were these two unassuming people? At one time they were among the West's best-known gamblers—Lottie Deno, as she was known in Texas, and her handsome, tough, knife-toting, half-Cherokee husband Frank Thurmond, a man whom many a western hero had considered a friend, including Doc Holliday.

Frank and Lottie were later immortalized in fiction by Alfred Henry Lewis, who captured their lives in his famous Wolfville novels. The series described the adventures of the citizens of the fictional town of Wolfville, set somewhere in Arizona. Wolfville was actually based on an assortment of towns on the Old Western Trail that crossed through New Mexico, including Tombstone and Gaylord, Arizona; Deming and Silver City, New Mexico; and Fort Griffin and San Antonio, Texas. Many of the stories are clearly set in the New Mexico and Texas locations where the events they are based on took place. Lewis's own favorite characters were Cherokee Hall and his true love Faro Nell, modeled on Frank Thurmond and Lottie Deno. They appear throughout the Wolfville series, which includes *Wolfville* (1897), *Sandburrs* (1900), *Wolfville Nights* (1902), *Wolfville Days* (1902), *The Black Lion Inn* (1903), *Wolfville Folks* (1908), and *Faro Nell and Her Friends* (1913), the final book in the series.

In 1896, Lewis traveled to Deming. Encouraged by Theodore Roosevelt and commissioned by publisher William Randolph Hearst, Lewis visited the Thurmonds at their ranch (located some forty miles east of Deming) and there refreshed his memory and gathered new information that he later wove into his works of fact and fiction.

When Frank Thurmond first knew Lewis on the frontier, Lewis was not using his famous pen name. To Frank and Charlotte, Lewis was their old cowboy friend Dan Quin. Dan had got acquainted with Frank and Charlotte at Fort Griffin, where Charlotte is known today in the folklore of the area as the mysterious lady gambler Lottie Deno. Because of trouble resulting from a killing, Frank used an alias at that time, calling himself Mike Fogarty.

The publication of this book is only possible because of the many people who, over the last ninety years, helped uncover the facts of Frank's and Lottie's lives and thereby preserved this valuable history. One such individual was J. Marvin Hunter, a young newspaperman who worked for the *Deming Headlight* in the early years of this century. He lived on a street behind the Thurmonds' home in Deming and learned of their identity. He became fascinated with their histories, and over the next fifty years, he collected as much information as he could. In 1957, he attempted to pull it together in a book. The title was to be "The Story of Lottie Deno: Her Life and Times." Unfortunately he was never to finish his research, and his last request was that his manuscript be completed and published. His children, however, did not work further on the manuscript but instead simply published their father's notes under his name.

In 1988, while traveling in the Texas hill country, my husband Steve and I visited the Frontier Times Museum, a small museum in the town of Bandera. On exhibition was an old trunk identified by a curled yellowing card that read, "This trunk once contained over $40,000 and belonged to the famous woman gambler Lottie Deno." We requested further information from the clerk, who sold us a copy of Hunter's book.

After reading the book, I realized that the story was only half told and that, as Hunter himself stated, "It would make an excellent story should the real facts be known." Although Hunter was unable to uncover all the facts, he preserved many clues that I was able to use in researching Lottie Deno's life more thoroughly.

Many people have attempted to write about Lottie Deno

but have based their accounts almost entirely on the work done by Hunter. By traveling to locations in Kentucky, New Mexico, and Texas, I made an effort to follow up the clues contained in other biographies and articles and to go further into the available documents to try to separate legend from fact. The most important source of new information turned out to be the old-timers still living in Deming who had known the Thurmonds. Interviews with these people and information housed in the Deming Luna Mimbres Museum helped me to fill in some of the gaps and made me confident that this account is more accurate and complete than any previous one. Yet I would hope that this book, like the one written by Hunter, will be but a stepping stone on the way toward a fuller account of the life of Lottie Deno.

Cynthia Rose
Santa Fe, New Mexico

Lottie Deno

Gambling Queen of Hearts

Chapter 1

Some forty miles southwest of Cincinnati and one hundred miles northwest of Lexington lies Warsaw, Kentucky, a river port settled in the mid-1770s. By 1840 it had grown into a center for the export of crops up and down the Ohio. It was here that Lottie Deno, christened Carlotta J. Thompkins, was born on April 21, 1844. According to what Lottie told friends and associates in her later years, her parents were well-to-do, and her father, in his later years, served in the Kentucky General Assembly. Lottie was devoted to her younger sister and took care of her financially during the years following the Civil War. It was Lottie's obligation to support her younger sister after the rest of her family died.

Lottie's father saw to it that his daughters attended one of the area's finest Episcopal convent schools, which was located near the family farm (or "plantation," as Lottie referred to it). The farm was actually closer to Lexington than to Warsaw. Since the early 1800s Lexington and Louisville had been agricultural and at the same time centers for trade with both the northern and southern states. The region was southern in character. The main crop was tobacco, which, along with hemp, was shipped north to Detroit and south to New Orleans. Horses were also traded, and racing was big business. The institution of slavery was well established in the Louisville area, as it was throughout the South.

As part of young Lottie's education, her father introduced her to worldly pursuits. He took her with him on business trips to New Orleans and Detroit and then to England and continental Europe. He sold his hemp to the shipbuilders of Detroit, sold his horses and tobacco abroad. He raced his horses mainly in New Orleans, where he indulged in his major vice. He was said by Lottie to have been an excellent gambler. He took Lottie to see some of the finest gambling establishments of the day. And he passed on to his daughter his skill at "pasteboards"—card playing, including many tricks of the trade.

In the 1850s, a trip to New Orleans for a young girl of twelve or thirteen must have been a marvelous adventure. Prosperous planters and businessmen of the period welcomed any excuse to board a southbound river packet. New Orleans was known in the 1850s as the "Good Time Town," the playground for Americans from the upper Mississippi. It was also known as the racing mecca of the nation—scarcely a place a husband would describe in detail to his pious wife.

Lottie's father owned slaves, and each of his daughters was assigned a nanny. Lottie's was a seven-foot-tall woman by the name of Mary Poindexter. Mary almost certainly accompanied Lottie and her father on their lengthy voyages, often traveling to various port cities along the river. The relationship between Lottie and Mary lasted long into Lottie's adult life, and many of the places they were introduced to on these trips would become more familiar to them one day.

At first glance New Orleans was probably both intrigu-

Few structures in Warsaw, Kentucky, survived the Civil War. This home, which still stands today, was typical of those existing around the time of Carlotta's birth in 1844. Photo by Steve Rose.

ing and depressing. Passengers arriving at the docks were confronted with unpleasant smells, rotting refuse, horse stables, mule yards, and the inhuman slave pens. For Mary, seeing the slave pens must have been painful—and a frightening experience for a young girl like Lottie. Lottie's father wanted his eldest child to know all aspects of the world that she would grow up to be a part of, to see cruelty and poverty as well as the prosperity of her own class.

The unsanitary condition of the docks was hardly noticed by the citizens of New Orleans, who must have considered it unavoidable, but the filth and stench obviously took their toll—the city had the highest death rate in the nation. The only relief for new arrivals was to seek out the nearest flower vendor and purchase sweet-smelling flowers to mask the disagreeable odors.

There was a pleasanter side to New Orleans. Lottie's father conducted business and found recreation at establishments such as the St. Charles Hotel and cafes like the Creole Orleans, Victor's, and the Cafe de Quatre Saisons. The enticing smell of food from fine restaurants could be a dangerous distraction for wealthy travelers, who were often easy prey for the numerous gangs of street children waiting to snatch a purse or pick a pocket.

Gambling was the type of entertainment preferred by Lottie's father. He would have had the option of visiting the Gem on Royal Street, the most elegant "drinking house" in the city, or placing bets at the Common Street Gallery, where men tried to shoot the flame off burning candles at twelve paces twenty times in succession. Bullfights, cockfights, dog races, and even rat races were held for the purpose of betting.

New Orleans had a strict curfew for ladies and slaves.

Lottie and Mary had to be in by eight o'clock or Mary could be arrested. A slave out on the street past curfew could be jailed and the owner fined. If the owner had insufficient money for the fine, he could "pay" by thrashing his slave at a rate of one penny per lash (up to three dollars' worth of lashes). With Lottie and Mary in their quarters, Lottie's father had the nights free for associating with his business friends.

Besides going to the casinos at night, Thompkins went to the Jockey Club and the Racing Club during the day. Trading and arranging for studs was carried on at these clubs. Racing was both a sport and a business for Lottie's father, a reputable breeder whose horses were known as winners.

Since Thompkins had no male children, he took his eldest daughter under his wing and taught her everything he could about the family business—at a time when girls were trained only in the social graces and the womanly household responsibilities they would be expected to assume. Lottie could not have guessed that what she was learning from her father would one day provide her with the means to survive.

Chapter 2

The Civil War began in 1861. The years preceding the war were characterized by bitter controversies regarding national economics and the issue of slavery. The South was dependent on its plantation agriculture, and by 1860 its economy was sustained by over four million slaves. The North, on the other hand, was more industrialized, and its farms were too small to be able to benefit from slave labor.

During the 1850s, the North wanted a protective tariff for its major industries, while the West wanted free farms for settlers and the building of roads, and the South wanted things left as they were. Thus, economic factors became mixed with the dispute over slavery. During the 1850s, from the 1854 Nebraska Act aiding western settlement to the Lincoln-Douglas debates on slavery in 1858, the nation became increasingly polarized. The 1859 attack on Harpers Ferry by abolitionist John Brown's group and the capture and execution of Brown and seven of the other attackers exacerbated the division between the northern and southern states.

Kentucky tried to remain neutral as long as possible, since it had social and economic ties with both the North and the South. Debates in the Kentucky General Assembly left the state divided on many questions, but there was a general desire to remain nonpartisan. In September 1861, however, Confederate troops invaded western Kentucky. Grant's army then moved in and occupied Paducah. The Kentucky legislature was thus pushed into creating a military force to join with Grant to drive out the southern army. This action aligned Kentucky with the Union for the remainder of the war. Many Kentuckians were sympathetic to the southern cause, however, and said good-bye to their families and left to join the Confederate army.

The Civil War proved disastrous for Lottie's family—as it did for so many southerners. Her father, for all his wide-ranging business interests, was a southerner to the bone. He bred horses, raced them in the South, owned slaves, and had a large farm that qualified as a plantation. In 1861, when Lottie was seventeen, her father enlisted in the Confederate army—never to return. Word came to the family that he was killed in the first fighting he was engaged in.

The shock of her husband's death was too much for Lottie's mother. She only had her daughters and a handful of faithful slaves who had remained with the family. Because of the Union army's blockade of southern ports, including those on the Ohio River near the family farm, food, clothing, and other basic necessities were at a premium. Lottie at seventeen was old enough to become head of the household when her mother's health began to fail. According to Lottie, however, other relatives were concerned about the influx of troops into the area and felt it wise to send young Lottie away.

Lottie, it was decided, would be sent to Detroit, where friends of the family would take her in. There were good southern families there, and Lottie might be able to find a suitable young man to marry who would return with her to Kentucky to take over the family business. The family gathered together what little money it had and gave it to Lottie for support during her stay in Detroit. Passage was arranged for Lottie and Mary Poindexter. The two arrived in Detroit sometime during the year 1861, and Lottie immediately entered into the social life of the city. She loved dancing, and night after night she attended social functions arranged for the young. For several months Lottie became completely preoccupied with social activities. Mary finally warned her that their funds were running low and would soon be gone. Lottie had been sent to Detroit for the purpose of acquiring a husband and was clearly failing in her mission.

How was Lottie Thompkins to support herself? The pampered young southern girl would have to grow up quickly. She did not relish getting a job, which would mean losing her social standing. At the time, gambling must have seemed a desperate measure, as well as a temporary one— the only way out of her predicament. When invited to visit a local gambling fraternity, Lottie accepted—not so much to be a guest as to participate. Lottie began to gamble to support herself and Mary, as well as her family back in Kentucky. She knew her mother and sister would be greatly shamed if they knew how she was managing. She sent home money to them but told them nothing. She felt that she could not return without a husband, and with every day that she stayed in Detroit the danger of her family learning about her gambling increased.

This account of Lottie's sojourn in Detroit is not the whole story. In later years she revealed to friends that part

Young Carlotta J. Thompkins as she looked in the 1860s. Photo courtesy of J. Marvin Hunter family.

of the reason she was sent to Detroit was to put distance between her and an undesirable suitor, Johnny Golden. A jockey who had once ridden for her father, he was two years younger than Lottie, but he had already served a term in the Confederate army. It appears that he either followed her to Detroit without her family's knowledge or arranged to meet her somewhere along the Mississippi. Like Lottie, Johnny was making a living as a gambler, and the two teamed up and gambled their way along the river.

Young Lottie faced a serious problem. Johnny was Jewish. If she returned to Kentucky with him, her family had informed her, she would not be welcome. Johnny Golden was from a rich Boston family. (Later accounts indicate he was from Georgia, but papers found in 1876 showed he was from Boston.) Lottie's family was not unusual in their prejudice. The climate in the country was growing more anti-Semitic by the day. Jews were now being threatened and killed throughout the North and the South. Even people calling themselves "abolitionists" and voicing opposition to slavery were turning their frustration and hatred upon the Jews.

During 1863, illegal trade in cotton contributed to the decline of the patriotic spirit on both sides of the conflict. This was especially evident in the cities and counties along the Mississippi. In 1860 and 1861, nearly 4,861,000 bales of cotton had been produced. Many of these sat rotting on the docks because the blockade on the river prevented sale and transport. As the southern forces were driven off the river, the Union armies occupied the evacuated cities and towns. Speculation and smuggling spread within Union ranks, and before long smuggling contaminated both armies. The Jews were blamed.

In January 1863, C. H. Dana, assistant to the secretary of

war, noted that "the mania for sudden fortune out of cotton, raging in a vast population of Jews and Yankees scattered throughout the country, has to a large extent corrupted and demoralized the army." This statement led General Grant himself to write, "I venture to say that no honest man has made money in West Tennessee in the last year, while many fortunes have been made in this time." He was so upset that he ordered all Jews out of his military district. Abraham Lincoln was angered by Grant's action and countermanded it, calling it an act of discrimination. Many northerners blamed the war on Jewish money that was believed to have financed the southern cause. Among the "proofs" cited was the fact that Jefferson Davis himself had appointed Judah P. Benjamin, a Jew, as his attorney general and retained him previously as secretary of war and secretary of state. New Orleans and many southern cities were home to well-established Jewish families. Since the founding of the country, they had shared the freedoms enjoyed by other Americans.

In the early 1800s, the growing anti-Semitism in Europe had spilled over into the United States. With the war as well as the poor state of the economy now being blamed on the Jews, the cry against them rose in volume, in both the North and the South, and conditions for Jews had worsened by the end of the war. They became the target of violent racial groups such as the Ku Klux Klan and were driven out of the South by terrorism. Many Jewish families, fearful for their safety, attempted to assimilate quickly, renouncing their religion.

Lottie had crossed an invisible boundary by teaming up with Johnny Golden. Lottie and Johnny may have gone to the family farm together before she left for Detroit, or Lottie may simply have told her family about her relationship with

Johnny. Whatever occurred, it was enough in those times to cause a family to disown its daughter. Certainly they would have done so had they known that she was living with him, unmarried, and making her living by gambling.

Lottie and Johnny, accompanied by Mary, continued their life of gambling on the river and remained together during the war. Young and in love, Lottie and Johnny made a commitment to their relationship. Eventually, however, Johnny began having difficulties, either because of the rampant anti-Semitism or bad luck with his gambling. He and Lottie decided to part company temporarily, and they chose San Antonio, Texas, as the place they would meet again. She and Mary were to go down the river to New Orleans and stay there until she had made enough money for the journey to Texas. Johnny did not tell her when he would come for her, but he expected he would be there before long.

Chapter 3

Lottie and Mary were now alone on the Mississippi traveling south to New Orleans. In 1864, the entire route was safe, since the war was almost over. The Union army had controlled the river during most of the war, and the towns along the banks were garrisoned with soldiers who manned gunboats patrolling the river between ports and aided the transport of goods to the northern states. During this period there was a high rate of desertion among both armies, and many men headed west, away from the fighting. A well-known sign placed strategically downriver read "Texas that way," with an arrow pointing west. Lottie would soon go there herself, but she first had to reach New Orleans.

Johnny knew Lottie and Mary would be better off without him. He had served in the Confederate army, was despised as a Jew, and, on top of everything, was a gambler, who could easily become involved in a fatal quarrel over cards. It is possible that he had already killed someone and was on the run. Later in life, he was wanted for at least one murder in Texas.

This era in American history was especially violent. America had been completely torn apart by the war. Bands of renegade soldiers from both armies roamed the South stealing and killing. They had lost all respect for human life and were concerned only for their own survival. The plantations had been destroyed, and former slaves seeking refuge huddled together in camps, which became targets for the hate groups that began to organize.

By the end of the war, Lottie's mother had died, and Lottie began sending money home to pay for her sister's education. Lottie hoped to win enough money to be able to send her sister to a fine boarding school and still have sufficient funds left over for the trip to Texas. So that her sister would accept the money she sent, Lottie wrote to her family that she had met and married a wealthy cattleman from Texas. She claimed the money she was sending was a gift from her generous husband and that he would send more should more be needed.

Lottie concocted this story to save face. She may have already known that she would never see any of her family again, but she needed them to think well of her. She also wanted to make sure that her younger sister would never have to resort to earning a living, but would have a proper life in Kentucky—the kind of life that Lottie had dreamed of before the war destroyed her family's fortunes. Although she had no contact with the family, it seems clear that they had been financially ruined by the war.

Not much is known about Lottie's days on the river. In her later life, however, Lottie did recount two incidents. One time, the boat Lottie and Mary were traveling on stopped along a sandbar in the river. Late in the evening, Lottie and Mary decided to take a walk. Lottie preceded Mary along the shoreline carrying her parasol and enjoying the evening air. Suddenly Mary's sharp eye spotted a large rattlesnake coiled and ready to strike her mistress. The tall, strong

Gallitan County docked a riverboat for restoration in 1989 on the Ohio River. It was in use during the period that young Lottie began her travels as a riverboat gambler. Photo by Steve Rose.

woman lunged forward and threw herself down on top of the reptile, saving Lottie from injury. Mary herself was bitten and became very ill. A finger had to be amputated, presumably to save her from spreading gangrene.

A second incident occurred when the two ladies were walking around the deck of the boat as it was docking to take on passengers. Two Union soldiers started to board. When one of the young men looked up and saw Lottie, he began to shout at her about cheating him in a card game upriver. He jumped on board and began to run at Lottie as if he intended to harm her. Mary stepped in front of Lottie. Her sheer size stopped the man. With her strong arms she picked up the soldier, lifted him over her head, and tossed him into the muddy water below.

During the winter of 1864–1865, Lottie remained in New Orleans. She gradually filled her trunks with the finest in Parisian fashions and indulged herself in what culture there was left in the city her father had first taken her to see. It was under military occupation but still retained its elegance and beauty.

The last battles of the war had been fought. On April 9, 1865, the war was declared over. Texas had been one of the states that had seceded in March 1861. More than fifty thousand Texans had left home to fight for the Confederacy. These men were on their way to Texas, along with many southerners who could not accept the consequences of the war. In the mid-1860s the giant cattle drives began, and many ex-soldiers joined these drives and came to be known as "cowboys."

Mary and Lottie set out for Texas in May 1865.

Chapter 4

San Antonio was Lottie and Mary's destination. In 1865, it was already a well-established city. It had been founded in 1718 by the Spanish, who had explored the area and driven out or suppressed the Indian population. It later fell under French rule and then Mexican rule, which essentially ended in 1835, when it was captured by the Texan army, although it was several times reoccupied by the Mexican army. The population was a mixture of the newly arrived Americans and the descendants of the Spanish and French and of the Africans who had been brought in as slaves.

For nearly two centuries the main plaza of San Antonio was reserved for the entertainment of the local citizens. The main activities were sports and gambling. Cards, games of chance, and betting in almost every form existed on the plaza. Both men and women gambled openly, and wagering was not restricted to the lower social orders. In fact, the governor of the city and other high public officials as well as local grandes dames were known to frequent public gaming booths to place bets.

The gaming booths were arranged around the plaza. Play went on day and night, although most of the activity occurred after sunset. Private games were also held at the

West side of Alamo Plaza, San Antonio. View from the Menger Hotel, in the 1860s. Photo courtesy of The Institute of Texan Cultures, San Antonio, Texas.

homes of some of the most distinguished residents. These games usually involved even higher stakes than were available at the public booths. After Texas declared itself a republic, a law was passed that the gaming tables on the plaza must be moved indoors or at least be housed under roofed pavilions.

When Lottie and Mary arrived, San Antonio had a population of over ten thousand, and with the end of the Civil War gambling was reaching an all-time high as wealth from ranching increased. In some of the indoor establishments, money was displayed in "piles and stacks," some of which towered several feet high. The gold and silver coins had to be scooped or shoveled into buckets or wheelbarrows to move them from table to table, and they were moved from casino to casino by oxcart and under heavy guard. Before the end of slavery, slaves had been gambled away, and sheep, goats, and sometimes entire cattle herds were placed as stakes.

Johnny Golden sent Lottie and Mary to wait for him in San Antonio, knowing that great fortunes could be made there. The two women arrived on June 1, 1865. They found lodgings at Mrs. Adams's Boarding House, where they settled for several months, venturing out only to the opera or to social gatherings of prominent San Antonians. It was only after Lottie had established her credentials among the higher social circles of the city that she entered her first gaming casino, on October 25, 1865. Lottie recollected later, in conversation with J. Marvin Hunter, that she initially went to the Cosmopolitan Club. Later she was offered a job at the University Club, which was owned by Frank Thurmond and his brothers Harrison and Bob. The three brothers were Confederate veterans who, along with their father J. C.

Thurmond and their younger sister Jenny, had come to San Antonio from Georgia to start a new life.

Lottie was hired at their club to deal cards for faro and other games. Faro, originally a French game, was a favorite in England among upper- class gamblers. Especially popular among ladies of the English gentry, this import gave additional "class" to Lottie's position at the club. As a dealer she was paid a percentage of the winnings and became conspicuously successful. Lottie continued to dress in the finest styles of the day. She and Mary soon rented a small adobe house on San Pedro Street, and later she bought a much larger home on Main.

Lottie never allowed smoking, drinking, or cussing at her tables. Mary always sat behind her on a stool. She acted as Lottie's lookout, keeping a careful watch on players who might be cheating or thinking of drawing a weapon. Lottie, however, was in less danger of violence than other players. Her dress and manner—an important element in her success—were designed to disarm suspicion. Lottie was given the title "Angel of San Antonio" by locals, who accepted her as the "lady" she was reared to be despite the fact that she was a "working woman."

The years passed and Johnny Golden still had not shown his face. Lottie's time in San Antonio afforded her the opportunity to take a long look back at her relationship with Johnny, the losses of the war, and the severance of ties with her family. As she developed into a mature woman who was used to being independent, she began to fall out of love with Johnny.

Lottie remained in San Antonio from 1865 to 1870. She is said to have had many suitors, but would have nothing to do with any of them—except for Frank Thurmond. Frank

Frank Thurmond. Photo taken in Denison, Texas, in the 1870s. Photo courtesy of J. Marvin Hunter family.

was the most dashing and adventurous of the Thurmond brothers, and he eventually took the place of Johnny Golden in Lottie's life.

Frank was over six feet in height, slender in build, but muscular. He wore his hair long at that time and had a large mustache and piercing blue eyes. He was part Cherokee but had been raised as a fine Georgia gentleman. He was a gambler and was adept at any game.

Because gambling was an accepted fact of life in San Antonio, no one ever suffered a decline in social status as a result of laying a wager. Gamblers did risk physical harm, however, and occasionally pistol or knife fights occurred. Frank Thurmond, who would give ground to no one, got into an altercation during a game and killed a man with his bowie knife. He fled San Antonio and stayed on the run for the next ten years. Strangely, there is no record of his having been wanted by the authorities. It is likely that the law was satisfied that the dead man had started the fight, but the dead man's family and friends may have put out a contract on Frank, forcing him to leave town.

Lottie had been having her own problems. After nearly six years, Johnny Golden finally showed up. He found Lottie dealing faro in the Thurmonds' club. As Lottie later told J. Marvin Hunter, she didn't see him enter, but she began to lose at the game she was playing. She felt his presence and turned around. There he was in the flesh—after all that time. Johnny soon learned about Frank. When Frank had to cut and run, Johnny tried to get Lottie to team up with him again, but it was Frank that she loved now.

Meanwhile, Mary Poindexter had become increasingly involved with the local community of freed slaves, and she began getting into street fights with gang leaders. San An-

tonio had several gangs run by women who took in or-
phaned children and taught them to steal as a way of
making a living. Some gangs were made up of African
Americans, others were predominantly Polish or Mexican.

Finally, Mary went her own separate way. She packed
her things one day and was gone. She and Lottie never saw
each other again.

With Frank out of the picture, Johnny Golden started
claiming Lottie was his wife. This undoubtedly helped Lottie make the decision to pack her own things and set out to
find Frank in West Texas. It seems that Frank had made her
some promises.

San Antonio in 1870, the year Lottie went to West Texas. Corner of
Alamo Plaza and Blum Street. Courtesy of The Institute of Texan
Cultures, San Antonio, Texas.

Chapter 5

Lottie arrived at Fort Concho, Texas, on the stage from San Antonio early in 1870. She immediately became the object of local gossip because women of her stature seldom got off the stage at the fort intending to stay.

Lottie rented a small house on the edge of town, at the end of Concho Avenue. She rested for only one day, then decked herself out in her finery and entered the local gambling establishment. Her beauty and graces were immediately noticed, as was her skill at cards.

Her mysterious arrival, her unusual profession, and her elegance and proper manner caused speculation that she was an aristocratic young woman from New Orleans who had run away from her strict home. Others believed she was a member of the European nobility and had come west to experience the American frontier. She certainly acted like a lady. Some of the locals, however, were not respectful and started to call her "Mystic Maud," a name that signified a doubtful reputation. She is known by that name in Fort Concho even today.

She gambled in Fort Concho for only a few months. Then she boarded the stage and left, unannounced and mysteriously, just as she had arrived. She first went to Jacksboro.

During the next two years she put in an appearance in several other towns in West Texas, including San Angelo, Dennison, and Fort Worth. Her movements lend credence to the story that she was looking or waiting for some man and that she rendezvoused with him at various locations. Lottie was known in Jacksboro as an unusual character. According to one writer, she was "cultured, attractive, red-headed, and . . . was off brand in her habits as well as in her profession. Bafflingly crooked at cards and disappointingly straight in more personal matters, she left everybody guessing as to where she had come from."

The opinion that she on occasion was not above cheating at cards surfaces more than once in her history, and it seems to be justified. Though as an expert card player she could expect to win a good percentage of the time, that was apparently not enough for a woman who depended on gambling for a living and expected to maintain the standard of elegance she had known from childhood. It was in Fort Griffin that Lottie got the name she is known by best. One evening she had taken on an opponent who was willing to play to the very end, even though Lottie was winning every hand. After the game was over, an old drunk shouted from the back of the saloon, "Honey, with winnings like them, you ought to call yourself Lotta Denero." At this suggestion, she began using the name Lottie Deno and from then on appears in records in West Texas under that name. It was convenient for her to acquire a new name. Lottie never used the name Thompkins during her gambling career—she wanted to prevent word of her doings from getting back to her home town in Kentucky.

Fort Griffin during this period was referred to as the "Sodom of the West." Its reputation was perhaps even worse than that of Dodge City, Kansas. Many of the West's most notorious desperados came to the Flats, an area of makeshift wooden buildings surrounding the actual fort, to visit the saloons, brothels, and gambling casinos, which provided everything from roulette, faro, and poker to pool. The population consisted mostly of young men who had fought for the Confederacy and who now suffered from a sense of displacement and alienation. Quite a number were criminals on the run. In the Flats they found a place of refuge and formed a community of sorts to protect their common interest in not being apprehended by the law.

Fort Griffin itself had been established in 1867. (It was initially called Camp Wilson but was soon renamed after Captain Charles Griffin.) Its purpose was to protect settlers and cattlemen from Kiowa and Comanche Indians and from roving gangs of white outlaws who were stealing cattle and burning out settlers.

The social climate at Fort Griffin was racially polarized. The troops stationed there were primarily black soldiers from the Union army who had been assigned to defend the western territory. (These soldiers were later known as buffalo soldiers; they were named this by the Indians, who saw a resemblance between the black, tightly curled hair of the soldiers and the hair of the buffalo.) The combination of Confederate veterans and black soldiers—freed slaves with the power of the army behind them—was bound to be an explosive one.

On top of that, living conditions at the fort were difficult. The original buildings were constructed of green lumber hauled from East Texas and from stands of trees near San Antonio. During the hauling, the dry climate of West Texas caused the wood to warp so severely that it had to be cut into shorter lengths than normal. The barracks, pieced together from this lumber, were more cramped than normal. A hut fourteen feet in length, eight feet in width, and five feet ten inches in height housed six men. It is no wonder that the soldiers were primed to drink, gamble, and fight whenever they were allowed to spend time in the Flats.

It was 1872 when Lottie got off the stage at Fort Griffin for the first time. She went about her usual routine of finding a place to live and settling in. She rented a small adobe house located at the periphery of the Flats. She retired to these quarters and remained there for several days before entering the Bee Hive, one of the local gambling houses. She soon became a regular.

Why would a woman who loved and could afford to buy beautiful clothing, had good manners, and possessed a refined beauty want to reside in a place like Fort Griffin when she could easily have lived in a more pleasant setting? Perhaps because of one of the bartenders at the Bee Hive, a fellow going by the name of Mike Fogarty. Mike Fogarty was in fact Frank Thurmond. It seems likely that Lottie, following his instructions and relying on infrequent letters, had gone from town to town supporting herself through gambling until she finally found him.

Lottie is said to have lived a secluded existence. The town documents do not indicate Lottie and Frank were especially close. This is understandable. After all, the two were hiding, Frank from the men who wanted him dead and Lottie from Johnny Golden.

Lottie, however, did vary her routine by making occasional excursions to neighboring towns. In the later part of the 1870s, Lottie visited Jacksb ro and met a young dentist there named Dr. John Henry Holl day. Doc Holliday had

John H. "Doc" Holliday. Photo courtesy of University of Oklahoma Library, Western History Collections.

heard about the wicked town of Fort Griffin and its gambling tables, and he decided it would be a good place for him, since he himself was in trouble with the law. Frank and Doc Holliday became friends in Fort Griffin. Historians have tried to link Doc and Lottie romantically, but both denied all such rumors. Doc undoubtedly found her beautiful and may have hoped for a more serious relationship, but Lottie's commitment to Frank Thurmond and Frank's reputation as a tough hombre were enough to give any prospective suitor serious pause.

Frank Thurmond didn't work steadily at the Bee Hive. He was in and out of Fort Griffin, herding cattle west along the trail to Arizona or riding shotgun on the stage line. Lottie was often left to her own devices.

Chapter 6

The best-known story involving Lottie Deno in Fort Griffin is a violent tale recorded in *The Quirt and the Spur* by Edgar Rye and in *Doc Holliday* by John Myers, among other places. Following is Myers's account:

It was during the time [Lottie] was dealing Faro in the Flats that a couple of tinhorn gamblers, known respectfully as Monte Bill and Smokey Joe, quarreled over a short card game. Each accused the other of cheating, and each was probably right. Each thought he could beat the other to the draw and each was only half right. There were two corpses on the floor when Sheriff Bill Cruger rushed in to take charge. Everybody that could had made tracks, with the exception of the redheaded Lottie, who was coolly counting her chips as the sheriff arrived. When the sheriff said that he couldn't understand why she had remained on the scene, she merely murmured, "But then you have never been a desperate woman."

In several versions of the story, the money that was on the table that night disappeared. Lottie was the only one left in the room, and most think she quietly slipped it into her purse, then left for the evening.

Rye provides a twist to the story in telling of an event that occurred prior to the gunfight. Benjamin Marks, known locally as "Cheap John," was a Jewish peddler who traveled the countryside selling pots and pans, tools, thread, and other essential items. Before the famous card game, John had been in Fort Griffin for about a week and had departed for the next community. Smokey Joe heard that the peddler had made quite a bit of money during his recent stop. Thinking that no one really cared about the Jewish peddler, Joe began to talk about how John had borrowed money from him and had never paid him back. He then said he was going to ride out after the old man and collect. The next afternoon Joe rode back into Fort Griffin wearing the old peddler's boots. Some of the townspeople asked Joe what had happened. Joe shrugged off their questions, merely saying that there had been trouble. Angered by his remarks, the townspeople searched Joe and found he had several other things belonging to the peddler. When pressed for the truth, all Joe would say is that he was forced to kill John in self-defense. According to one version, Joe was hung for the offense, but he was not. He was killed by Monte Bill.

Over the years Lottie may have become hardened to such violent events or at least resigned to witnessing them. It would have been important to her to appear strong, regardless of her feelings. As an independent woman she could not afford to show signs of weakness.

Like many of the other townspeople, Lottie probably had little respect for Smokey Joe and might even have been glad to see him finally pay for his crimes.

The years Lottie spent in Fort Griffin were a period of transition and waiting. According to several local people, Lottie claimed that her husband had gone west to find land

and would send for her when he had made his purchase. Lottie was apparently resigned to living in a town like Fort Griffin and making her living as a gambler if it meant that she and Frank would eventually be able to start a life together elsewhere.

Although Lottie did love drama and relished her success in gambling, Fort Griffin must have been a dismal experience, especially compared with San Antonio, where she had established herself among the social elite and bought a fine home. Even in San Antonio, though enjoying a freedom and independence that few women of the time achieved, Lottie never lost sight of her ultimate goal—a "respectable" married life in the kind of social setting she remembered from girlhood. She must also have been concerned about security in her later years. Lottie was already in her early thirties and could not expect to remain a "gambling queen."

Frank Thurmond may have seemed an odd choice to provide the kind of life she wanted. Though raised as a southern gentleman, he had a become a man of the Wild West—a restless cowboy, gambler, and adventurer, as well as a dangerous man with a knife.

Frank was said to carry his bowie knife in a leather sheath hung on a leather strap down his back in such a way that he could easily reach the knife by raising his hand to the back of his collar. It is likely that Frank taught this trick to his friend Doc Holliday, a fellow Georgian. Frank had got himself in trouble with it in San Antonio, and Doc later used it in an incident in Fort Griffin that nearly cost him his life.

In 1872, when Lottie was establishing herself in West Texas, a young man by the name of John C. Jacobs first came to Fort Griffin. Jacobs, who was only twenty, was born in Gallatin County, Kentucky, the county Lottie was from.

Soon after his arrival in Fort Griffin, Jacobs filed to become sheriff, was accepted for the appointment, and remained in that position for many years.

About this time another young adventurer came to Fort Griffin. Dan Quin, like Jacobs, had been influenced by the stories of the frontier and had decided to leave his home in Ohio and sign on as a cowhand on regular drives along the Chisholm Trail to Kansas. Later he would work on the Western Trail that led to Arizona.

As mentioned in the introduction, Quin later changed his name to Alfred Henry Lewis and wrote a series of books about his adventures and the adventures of those he had met as a young man riding the trails.

Both Jacobs and Lewis wrote about an incident that involved Lottie, Frank, and Doc Holliday. In Lewis's account, Doc Holliday and Cherokee Hall (Frank) are playing cards in a saloon called the Red Light. Faro Nell (Lottie) is sitting behind Cherokee. The game is high-card faro.

". . . I'll do better than that," returns Cherokee, as he snaps the deck in the Faro Box, "I'll let you fix the limit to suit yourself. Make it the ceilin' if the spirit moves you."

"That's generous!" says Holliday.

The game begins and the stakes reach as high as $30,000. Before too long Holliday has won every dime, and Faro Nell, who is acting as Cherokee's lookout, is steaming mad about the losses.

As Cherokee rises, Faro Nell slides off the lookout's stool and into the vacated chair. When Cherokee loses

"*Faro Nell*" *from the book* Faro Nell and Her Friends, *illustrated by* Marchand.

the last bet I hears Nell's teeth come together with a click. I don't dare to look towards her at the time; but now, when she turns the box back, takes out the deck, riffles and returns it to its place I give her a glance. Nell's as game as Cherokee. As she sets over against this licky invalid her color is high an' her eyes like two stars.

"An' now you've got to break me," says Nell to this Holliday. "Also, we restores to status as Colonel Sterett says in that Coyote paper, an' the limit retreats to an even hundred dollars. . . ."

The deal begins. Nell is winner from the jump; she takes in three bets to lose one plumb down to the turn. This Holliday calls the turn for the limit, an' loses. The cards go into the box again an' a next deal ensues. So it continues; and Nell beats Holliday hard for half an hour.

Nell wins back all the money that Cherokee has lost to Holliday.

"There, Cherokee," says Nell, an' thar's a soft smile an' a sigh of deep content goes with the observation,"there's your bank again; only it's thirty thousand stronger than it was four hours ago."

In 1928, J. Marvin Hunter received a letter in response to a query about this incident. He had asked John C. Jacobs if he remembered such a game. Jacobs replied as follows:

I remember well one such instance where a lot of money changed hands, and Lottie Deno coming out about three thousand dollars ahead, winning it all from Doc Holliday at the Bee Hive. It seems that Holliday had won over three thousand dollars and the layout [faro board] from Mike Fogarty, who operated the gambling

"Cherokee Hall" from the book Wolfville, *illustrated by Frederic Remington.*

resort, when Lottie Deno, who was lookout for Fogarty, proposed to Holliday that she be given a chance to recoup Fogarty's losses. Holliday agreed to this and the game was resumed, with a fifty dollar limit. The game did not last very long, for Lottie Deno copped every bet, and left Doc Holliday completely strapped.

Frank was later to tell folks that his favorite story in the Wolfville series, printed in *Cosmopolitan* magazine in 1897, was this tale of reversal of fortune. Lottie, however, was displeased by Lewis's portraits of her in the Wolfville stories, which did not fit her view of herself as a lady of good breeding.

Chapter 7

A large beehive was painted on the wall of the Bee Hive Saloon in Fort Griffin, and hanging above the door was this poem:

Within this Hive, we are alive;
Good whiskey makes us funny.
Get your horse tied, come inside;
And taste the flavor of our honey.

There were several saloons, dance halls, and gambling houses of distinction in Fort Griffin. The finest of these was the Cattle Exchange, which was directly across from the Bee Hive. The owner of the Beehive, John Shaunessey, was also co-owner of the Cattle Exchange, which Lottie never frequented. She remained a house gambler at the Bee Hive, where she was known as "Queen of the Pasteboards," for two to five years (accounts vary). In San Antonio, where more women gambled, she dealt faro most frequently. Fort Griffin was a man's town, and there she usually dealt poker.

Lottie's schedule was the same whether Frank was in town or off on a journey. She left her house at nine o'clock every evening to go to the Bee Hive, where she would gamble late into the night. She would return home and sleep through

51

the morning, not opening her drapes until late afternoon.

She had one very good friend, the wife of an officer stationed at the fort. The two women would take rides in the countryside or travel to the nearby town of Albany, which was growing rapidly. Lottie would always be back in her small house before sunset.

Doc Holliday, after his arrival in Fort Griffin in 1876, also frequented the Bee Hive. He was known to go to the other clubs, but the Bee Hive was his usual hangout. And it was in the Bee Hive that Doc met the woman he'd later link up with, Kate Fisher, known as "Big Nose Kate." She was somewhat lacking in social graces, although it is said she had attended a fine girls' school before running off to the West. Kate followed Doc for many years, including the time he spent in Arizona with his friend Wyatt Earp, whom he met at the Bee Hive through John Shaunessey.

Lottie had become well established as the elegant lady gambler of Fort Griffin and the main attraction at the Bee Hive. When Kate came to town, Kate's attraction to Doc made her anxious to chase off any possible competition. According to several historians, Kate and Lottie had heated words one night over Doc. After Kate and Doc had made it known they were a team, Kate began to show her jealousy of anyone who might take Doc away from her. One evening Kate accused Lottie of trying to steal his affections. The accusation brought Lottie to her feet:

> "Why you low down slinkin' slut!" shouted Lottie. "If I should step in soft cow manure, I would not even clean my boot on that bastard! I'll show you a thing or two!" Lottie pulled a gun, and Kate also drew a weapon. Doc Holliday placed himself between the two women.

This account makes it clear that both women were prepared to use their guns. One can imagine this juicy story becoming more and more colorful in the retelling. Certainly crude language and drawing a gun in an argument were not Lottie's style, but we can't know how she behaved in a quarrel or how serious the provocation may have been. There was some exchange of words that night—that much is clear, and Lottie left no doubt about her feelings for Doc Holliday. Kate could have him.

It was at the Bee Hive that Wyatt Earp and Doc Holliday were first introduced. Earp was then marshal of Dodge City and was looking for a fellow by the name of Dave Rudabaugh. Shaunessey told Earp that Doc Holliday could give him information about the location of the gang riding with Rudabaugh. Shaunessey introduced the two, who did not like each other at first. Doc agreed to get the information for the marshal. This meeting took place in mid-November of 1877, a few months after Lottie Deno had departed Fort Griffin. Doc went out into the Flats and found out the information that Earp needed. Earp then rode west to Fort Davis after Rudabaugh and his gang.

While Earp was away, Doc got himself into trouble with the local vigilante committee. The incident was recorded in Wyatt Earp's autobiography. Doc was playing cards with a fellow by the name of Bailey, who was known for always monkeying around with the "deadwood," the unsavory types who hung out in the saloon. Doc finally got fed up with Bailey's cheating:

> Doc called and Bailey spread down three kings. Doc didn't say a word but just quietly pulled down the pot and threw his hand away without showing what he held.

Of course Bailey started a big holler. I saw you palming one of those kings," said Doc. "Give me that money," roared Bailey. "I won it and I'll have it."

Doc was stacking the chips in front of him as Bailey reached for them. Doc knocked his hand away. Bailey went for his six-shooter and was coming up with it when Doc drew a long knife from under his coat collar—he had it hanging by a cord down his back—and with a side-swipe below the brisket ripped Bailey wide open. Doc was arrested.

Bailey died. Doc was taken to the hotel, where he was held by the town marshal and two police deputies. Bailey's cowboy and town friends gathered outside the hotel and began forming a lynch mob. Their shouts were getting uglier. They started talking about hanging Doc before morning.

Kate got word of Doc's situation and went to work figuring out a plan. First, she went to see Doc where he was being held. She had a short visit and then left. She ordered a couple of horses from the livery stable and had them hitched in the alley. Then she set a fire blazing in a shed behind the hotel. She ran into the street yelling "fire" and watched as the crowd rushed to the burning building and deserted the front of the hotel.

Kate was wearing men's clothing and was carrying a satchel. She pulled out two six-shooters and forced the guards to release Doc. Doc disarmed the guards, and Doc and Kate backed out of the hotel door, mounted the two horses hitched in the alley, and rode north to Dodge City, some four hundred miles away.

Chapter 8

Perhaps the most disturbing event in the life of Lottie Deno occurred in Fort Griffin. Johnny Golden, the man she had first loved, had found where she was living and came looking for her to try to win her back. Unfortunately for Johnny, she had spent too many years in San Antonio waiting for him. Though she had maintained her self-respect as an independent woman, Lottie had always wanted someone to take her away from gambling and give her a good name and decent life. Frank had promised her this, and she had made a commitment to him, believing he would stand by his word. She could not consider returning to someone like Johnny, who, taken his promises so lightly and now was even wanted by the law for murder. She had made her decision long before to let go of the past.

In October 1876, Johnny Golden killed a man. His name appears in "A List of Fugitives from Justice," issued by the governor in 1876. Johnny had fled the scene but was captured and arraigned for the murder in February 1877. He was able to escape, however, and in April Johnny headed toward Fort Griffin, intending to win Lottie back and take her away with him.

Frank was in Silver City, New Mexico Territory, where new silver strikes had been made. He had written Lottie that he would get settled, then send for her. Although Frank had stuck by her thus far—often from a distance—Lottie may have wondered whether he would keep his word and be willing to settle down. Frank, like Johnny, had killed a man, and he was wild, restless, and always dreaming of adventure. He laughed at danger—thought nothing of riding shotgun on the stage through Indian territory during some of the roughest times.

Meanwhile, Lottie had received another letter from Frank. He was doing a little prospecting and a lot of gambling. He wanted to know whether she would join him now. After receiving this letter, Lottie went to Sheriff Jacobs, ostensibly to ask for advice. Jacobs described the visit:

Lottie Deno came to me on one occasion and told me she needed a friend in whom she could confide, and asked me for my advice on a matter that revealed to me that she was no ordinary woman. She told me her real name (it was not Lottie Deno), but pledged me to never reveal it to anyone as long as I live, and I have kept that promise even to this late day. She stated that she was born in Kentucky, and that her parents were well-to-do prominent people there. Her father was well known in the 1860's as one of the outstanding turfmen of the Blue Grass State, and owned a string of blooded race horses which made all the race centers of that day, New Orleans, Louisville, Kansas City, Chicago and St. Louis, and one of his winning horses was a thoroughbred that won in many of the sweepstakes. His chief jockey was a young man who was a fine rider, but the profligate son of a Georgia father, whose gambling and wild ways kept him involved in trouble of one kind or another. In 1860,

Lottie, contrary to the wishes of her parents, married this jockey, and was therefore disowned by them, and they would never allow her to enter their home afterwards. Her letters to her mother would always be returned unopened, and they never forgave her for marrying against their wishes. For several years she and her husband, who was a professional gambler, drifted around over the country, living in Kansas City, New Orleans, Mobile, Nashville, and other centers where gambling flourished. He taught Lottie all the tricks of the card sharp, and she became an expert in flipping the pasteboards herself. The day came, some months before she came to Fort Griffin, when her husband killed a man with a knife during a card game, took nearly all the cash Lottie possessed, told her he was going to Mexico, and left her almost destitute.

According to Jacobs, Lottie said to him, "Mr. Jacobs, I have just received a letter from my husband. He has located me here, and says for me to join him in San Angelo and go west with him, to Arizona or California, where we will make a new start. I am afraid to go to him. Please advise me what to do."

It is not entirely clear why Lottie told Jacobs this bizarre combination of lies and half-truths, except that she was evidently planning to leave Fort Griffin and wanted to make sure she left no trail that would lead to Frank Thurmond. Frank was still very likely in danger because of the killing in San Antonio. There is no evidence that Lottie ever married Johnny Golden or that her family totally disowned her and returned her letters. It is important to note that Jacobs was from her home county and very likely knew of her family. She may have wanted people to believe—if word got back to Kentucky—that she was at least respectably married, even if to a "profligate son" and a Jew to boot. And it may have been her love of drama that made her create such an elaborate tale of woe. There are no simple answers.

Within weeks after Lottie had gone to Sheriff Jacobs, Lottie's past caught up with her. Jacobs received news of the arrival of a fugitive in Fort Griffin—Johnny Golden. It seems Johnny was going around town inquiring about Lottie Deno.

Jacobs called Lottie in for questioning. She told him that Johnny was a man "who knew her husband's troubles." Jacobs believed her. He thought Johnny was not of the same class as Lottie, perhaps because of Johnny's Jewish last name or because of his looks. Lottie told Jacobs that "she had known Johnny Golden elsewhere." Jacobs observed that somehow "the mention of Golden made her uneasy," and he could tell that Johnny held "some kind of club over her head." Jacobs says that he "sent her away without any further questioning, satisfied with her answer."

A few hours later, Johnny was picked up by Marshal Bill Gilson for a minor infraction of the local law, and Gilson and Deputy Draper began escorting him to the post guardhouse up on the hill. As the group approached the wagon yard behind one of the saloons owned by Shaunessey, gunfire suddenly started up. When the shooting was over Johnny Golden lay dead in the street.

There are two versions of what really happened. Marshal Gilson claimed that Golden had tried to escape and was shot down in the confusion. According to a second version, several men belonging to a gang that had ridden in with Golden ambushed the marshal and the deputy in an attempt to free Golden. Golden was killed in the melee. In any case

Johnny Golden, the young jockey Lottie had once loved, lay shot and slain.

When the news reached Lottie, she experienced a shock. Talk was that she blamed herself for the killing. And it is said that she was inconsolable for a time. She bought a suit of clothes for the burial and paid for a coffin, which totaled $65. She went home. She didn't join the funeral procession that took Johnny to Boot Hill that day. She stayed in her house with the curtains drawn.

Chapter 9

The body of Johnny Golden lies in Fort Griffin cemetery. For Lottie, an important part of the past would
always remain there.

It wasn't long after Johnny's death that Lottie began
making arrangements to leave Fort Griffin. Once again Lottie confided in her friend Sheriff Jacobs. Jacobs had brought
from Kentucky a small leather trunk commonly made in
that state. It must have caught Lottie's eye the first time she
saw it because she went to Jacobs and asked if she might buy
it. Jacobs offered to give it to her, but she insisted on paying
him. Lottie told Jacobs that she planned to leave Fort Griffin
within a few days and that she was going west to join her
husband. She said they would possibly go to California to
start a new life.

Lottie left town on May 25, 1877. She waited for the Fort
Concho stage a mile south of town, her only luggage the
leather trunk. It was nearly a month since Johnny's murder
and burial. According to Jacobs, Lottie seemed to leave "that
hellhole Fort Griffin" with few regrets.

The rent on her house had been paid for the month, so
no one bothered to enter immediately. When they did go in
they found the small one-room adobe lavishly furnished.
Even in this small roughneck town, Lottie never gave up her

Lottie Deno as she looked at Fort Griffin, Texas, in the 1870s. Photo courtesy of Fort Concho National Historic Landmark, San Angelo, Texas.

Sheriff John C. Jacobs in the 1920s. Photo courtesy of J. Marvin Hunter family.

desire for elegant surroundings. Pinned to the bed pillow was a note that read, "Sell this outfit and give the money to someone in need of assistance."

The mysterious Lottie Deno, who had gambled with some of the West's most notorious men, had finally moved on, leaving behind a legend that persists in the popular imagination to this day.

Local historians hint at a dark side to her life at Fort Griffin. According to one document, she was fined a hundred dollars for operating a house of prostitution, and it has been said that she "was a wicked, ugly woman, herself a prostitute." Although the allegation that she ran a whore-house has been widely circulated, the preponderance of evidence contradicts it. The fine may have been imposed because as house gambler she had some business responsi-bilities. Lottie would have been held responsible for any-thing that happened under the gambling house roof.

The charge that she was a prostitute may also stem from the fact that she did often help prostitutes financially and in other ways. Later in her life she spoke of trying to encourage them to get out of the business and start new lives. The conditions of frontier life must also have contributed to suspicions about Lottie. In frontier towns there were few opportunities besides the business of prostitution that al-lowed a woman to become independent and prosperous — and gambling and prostitution were linked in most people's minds.

Another local account tells of her having been involved with the saloon owner John Shaunessey. It is unlikely that Lottie would have preferred Shaunessey to Frank, and Frank's reputation was sufficient to keep any prudent man from paying court to his lady love.

In her book *Interwoven*, Sallie Reynolds Matthews, a well-respected Fort Griffin local, states that she had "never heard of any reproach against [Lottie Deno's] character other than her gambling, though she was shunned by the better classes." Even this last assertion must be qualified. Sheriff Jacobs knew of Lottie's close friendship with the wife of an officer stationed at the fort. For the wife of a military officer to keep company with a woman of "ill character" would have been unlikely, since her husband would suffer reproach as a result. It seems clear, however, that except for this friend, Lottie lived a comparatively isolated existence in Fort Griffin—both because of the gambling and her need to preserve secrecy to protect herself and Frank.

Jacobs is quoted as saying that Lottie was "gracious, fine in her breeding, and had good manners which were shown at all times." Jacobs wrote about Lottie's character in a letter to J. Marvin Hunter. According to Hunter, Jacobs "never saw Lottie Deno take a drink of liquor of any kind. And he last saw Lottie in El Paso, Texas in the year 1892, where she told him she had quit gambling, had married a New Mexico ranchman, joined the church and had settled down to a peaceful life."

Chapter 10

Lottie Deno left Texas and surfaced again in the mining town of Kingston, New Mexico, where she joined Frank Thurmond. He had been in New Mexico nearly a year.

Within the next few months Frank and Lottie set up a little gambling room at the back of the Victorio Hotel in Kingston, which was then in the midst of a boom because of local strikes in silver and gold. In Silver City they also set up at a saloon, a fine establishment called the Gem.

In 1878, mining mania had spread throughout most of the region surrounding Silver City. Frank and Lottie were taking advantage of it, buying and selling claims, buying real estate, and collecting on debts owed them from poker games. Word got around that a cowboy by the name of George W. Lufkin had, while prospecting, picked up a piece of high-grade ore in the area just south of Hillsboro and Kingston known as the Lake Valley region. Lufkin and another cowboy went back to the area in August 1878 to sink a few holes. They quickly discovered a vein of the same high-grade ore almost at surface level.

Like many others, these cowboys-turned-miners couldn't raise enough money for a grubstake. They were eventually grubstaked by John A. Miller, a trader at Fort Bayard, near

Early mining camp in the Lake Valley Mining District near Cooke's Peak.
Photo courtesy of Deming Luna Mimbres Museum.

Riley George's burros carrying water to sell to the miners in the Cooke's Peak area. Riley, who owned a ranch near Deming, was said to have turned a bigger profit than the miners. Photo courtesy of Deming Luna Mimbres Museum.

Silver City, and they soon returned to the mining area. While Lufkin and his partners, rancher McEvert and cowhand Chris Watson, continued their digging, Miller negotiated with eastern investors. Eventually an engineer named George Daly was brought in to survey the strike. He was known for his work in the Leadville, Colorado, area. Daly's reports were favorable, and the land in Lake Valley was bought for $300,000. When news of the find spread, the Lake Valley region was inundated by prospectors from all over the world.

Many of these men needed to be grubstaked, and those who had already made a little money from mining operations had to be entertained at the poker tables. Frank and Lottie were happy to cater to both types of need. They grubstaked miners and gambled with them for their strikes or for part interest in their claims.

After Lottie arrived in New Mexico, Frank called her his wife by common law. She took his name and was known as Mrs. Frank Thurmond. This arrangement must have been a disappointment for Lottie. Although common-law marriage was not unusual in the West, it did not offer the kind of respectability she had been raised to believe in. Within two years the situation changed, however.

In 1856 a law had been enacted that forbade "living together or common law marriages." Law 916–917 for Crimes and Offenses, dated February 26, 1856, gave jurisdiction to courts in the territory of New Mexico to rule in matters of cohabitation. It was on the books in 1865 and was still on the books in 1915. The law read as follows:

> 916. The justice of the peace of the different counties of this Territory, are hereby authorized to punish those

At the right is Charlotte Thurmond, as she was called, in Silver City, New Mexico, in the year 1883, at Broadway and Main. Photo courtesy of Silver City Museum.

persons who come within the purview of the provisions of the following sections, which persons shall be tried upon an accusation made by any person before the proper judge.

917. Any person or persons who shall after the approval of this act, be found living together publicly as if they were married, and not being so, shall be considered as living in a state of concubinage, and shall be required immediately to contract and join in the bonds of matrimony, if there shall be no impediment to prevent their so doing; and if they do not form such union on the first requirement of any justice, and persist in their accustomed mode of life, they shall, on accusation thereof before any of the said justices, be fined in any sum not less than twenty-five dollars nor more than eighty dollars, for every time they shall be so found: PROVIDED, that if there be any impediment to prevent marriage of the persons aforesaid, and they do not separate, after having been required so to do, for the first time by any of the aforesaid justices, they shall on conviction thereof, on accusation, be fined for each violation of this act, in any sum not exceeding that above provided in this section, recoverable on execution as in civil cases.

As more people settled in New Mexico following the gold and silver strikes, there was some outcry over the condition of public morals. In 1880 counties and individual cities responded by enacting the same law. Hundreds of Grant County residents, including Frank and Lottie, flocked to the courthouses and to the churches.

The marriage register in Silver City, in section T, contains the following registration of marriage:

Thurmond, Frank; Silver City; Carlotta J. Thompkins; Silver City; December 2, 1880; presiding Issac Greives, J.P.P. No. 3; David Ebi & P.N. H. McMillian, (witnesses).

Grant Co. Clerk record

Lottie was by this time thirty-six years old. Frank and Lottie had been romantically involved since her days of dealing faro in San Antonio—about fifteen years.

Frank continued to stake miners' claims and reap the rewards. On July 28, 1880, Frank paid $2,000 into a deed filed with W. Malsted for one undivided half-interest in Malsted's mining claim in the Lone Mountain District of Grant County. Frank became part owner in this claim first filed by Malsted, who named the mine the Perseverance Mine. It was located in the same area as the Raspberry Mine and the Little Maud.

Frank made another investment in 1882, right after news spread of the biggest strike in the history of New Mexico. A chamber had been struck during the drilling of a shaft in the Lake Valley region (in the area surveyed by Daly) and had been sold to eastern financiers. A man by the name of John Levitt had a shaft-sinking contract with the Sierra Grande/ Plata companies, which had been formed to develop the strike.

The chamber was beneath only four feet of soil and some twenty feet of limestone. At this depth the ore began to assay out at forty ounces per ton. The light that penetrated the chamber the day of the strike was said by witnesses "to glitter along the crystals and calcite deposits," and the

Lake Valley ghost mine, remains of the silver chamber, Bridal City area. Photo by Steve Rose, 1993.

Early Deming, New Mexico. Gold Avenue, between 1890 and 1899. Photo courtesy of Deming Luna Mimbres Museum.

chamber was therefore named the Bridal Chamber. No one realized just how much ore there was, but it was a big enough strike that Frank Thurmond wanted a way in. The Bridal Chamber in its lifetime yielded millions of dollars in silver ore.

Frank had mining fever. He found the right miner to grubstake or to indulge in the right card game, and for $500 he was sold a one-third interest in the Black Crook, a mine located in the Bridal City Mining District. The claim record was filed in the clerk's office on November 27, 1882. In the deed agreement he agreed to work the mine and make improvements.

Frank must have done well in his mining ventures in the early 1880s. By June 1882, Lottie had purchased the Broadway Restaurant in Silver City. She sold it by October of that same year but continued to manage it. It was recorded in the paper that she invested her profit and other money in a hotel property in Santa Rita. And she also began to use her wealth to aid those in need. In September 1882, Lottie furnished board for the city prisoners.

By 1883 Frank had purchased a wholesale liquor house in the newly developing city of Deming. He also bought a lot (number 12, in block number 6) fronting Pine Street—a choice location. The date on the deed is July 6, 1885. This lot would one day be the site of Frank and Lottie's home. Frank had also purchased a ranch some forty miles east of Deming, near the Dona Ana Mountains.

Because of the new wealth from mining in the area, Deming was no longer a quiet little frontier town. It started as a tent city during construction of the railroad. Gradually saloons, stores, and finally residences began to appear throughout the city area.

Silver Street, Deming, in the early 1900s. Photo courtesy of Deming Luna Mimbres Museum.

Parade along Silver Street, Deming, early 1900s. Photo courtesy of Deming Luna Mimbres Museum.

One of the finest hotels between Los Angeles and Kansas City was the Harvey House built in Deming in 1881 by the railroad. The line that ran to Deming from Albuquerque was part of the Atchison, Topeka and the Santa Fe. In 1882, a railroad was built between Silver City and Deming, bringing more growth for both cities.

Lottie in Kingston, New Mexico, with unknown child. 1880s. Photo courtesy of J. Marvin Hunter family.

Chapter 11

Shortly after Frank and Lottie moved to Deming, an incident occurred that was a turning point in Frank's life. Frank owned a local Deming business and he and Lottie had a home. He was well respected in the region around Silver City and Deming although he still associated with the local gamblers. On August 29, 1884, the *Silver City Enterprise* reported the following:

If Deming is not a sensational town it is nothing. Without a weekly sensation the people are morose and sulky, and consider that the angel that hovers in the look-out chair is not on duty. On Wednesday night Dan Baxter, we learn, aggravated Frank Thurmond into a quarrel which resulted in Baxter's getting badly cut in the abdomen. We did not learn the particulars farther than that Baxter threw a billiard ball at Thurmond and provoked the trouble. Frank Thurmond has always been known as an inoffensive citizen here, while Baxter had the reputation of being very quarrelsome.

Frank may have been an "inoffensive citizen," but he evidently still carried a knife inside his shirt collar and had a quick temper. In the same column, the rest of the story is told:

Dan Baxter, the man cut by Frank Thurmond last week in a quarrel at Deming, died at that place on Tuesday night, from the effects of his injury. The affair is a very unfortunate one and the friends of both parties very much regret the occurrence. The newspapers published there for the purpose, we suppose, of disseminating news at the request of the friends of the parties, suppress the matter, not giving even the facts connected with the affair. Both men are well known in Silver City and throughout the territory and the facts would be of general interest and would not necessarily prejudice any fairminded person.

Perhaps because of this tragedy, Frank and Lottie gave up gambling. Frank put all his energies into land investing, mining, and cattle ranching. Frank had kept his word to Lottie. He had (under pressure from the law) given her his name in marriage. The gambling was finally over, and he provided her with material comforts. But Frank continued his independent life. He spent much of his time at the ranch or on mining trips, while Lottie lived in town—where she preferred to be.

The Deming home was probably the most important of the material comforts Frank provided for her. Lottie lived there most of the time and became an active member of the community. Resuming the kind of life she had been accustomed to in Kentucky before the war, she furnished her house elegantly and left the money-making entirely to Frank. She developed close relationships with neighbors and members of the local Episcopal mission church.

After joining the church, Lottie became involved with other Deming residents in supporting the construction of a new building to house St. Luke's Episcopal. St. Luke's was

*St. Luke's Episcopal Church in the early 1900s. Photo courtesy of
Deming Luna Mimbres Museum.*

one of Deming's earliest established missions. Its pastor, Reverend Dunlop, was the missionary bishop for a very large district, including Arizona and Indian territory. The first services, held in 1884, were conducted in the homes of congregation members. Charlotte Thurmond is listed in church documents as one of the founding members and as having helped to create the first Sunday school, along with Mary Hudson, H. D. Green, Clara L. Shepard, Laura A. Hall, Flora Ried, Henry Rathel, Roy Whitmore, R. D. Sidey, and Susie Tidmore.

Frank and Lottie had no children of their own, but they became "Aunt Lottie" and "Uncle Frank" to the children of Deming. Frank was not active in Lottie's church, but he did join the Odd Fellows, a fraternal organization dedicated to service to one's fellow man. Frank expanded his investments in mining. In partnership with James Martin, he purchased several mines located in the Tres Hermanas District south of Deming. For $10,000, they bought the following mines: the Crawford, Golconda, Monarch, Fraction, Song Bird, Zulu, Sultan, Homestead, Pole Star, Flat Foot, and Village Smith. These mines were probably purchased for later resale to eastern investors, since the area was known not for high-grade ore but primarily for base metals.

In any event he did not retain his substantial interest in these mines for long. Within the next two years Frank drew up a deed with Helen Lindauer, a neighbor and close friend of his and Lottie's. He sold her a half-interest in these mines for the sum of one dollar. The reasons behind this act are not known—but Frank and Lottie had a reputation for generosity.

Although Frank had become a respected citizen locally, he had one much publicized brush with the law. In 1893,

The Deming National Bank, which was "robbed" by Frank Thurmond.
Photo courtesy of the Deming Luna Museum.

during the week of the annual bank examiner's visit, Frank had $1,100 in his account at the Deming National Bank. The examiner, while counting the bills and other cash on hand, noticed one bill that was badly mutilated, even partly burned. He was satisfied with his overall inspection, however, and passed the bank for another year.

The examiner stayed in Deming for the night, then traveled to Silver City to inspect that city's bank. During that night, the Deming banker sent a messenger to Silver City with the Deming funds to place them in the Silver City bank in time for the next day's inspection. When the examiner arrived and began to count the cash, he noticed the mutilated bill he had seen the day before. He immediately realized that the banks were short, so he closed both of them and froze all accounts.

When Frank heard about the examiner's ruling, he reacted instantly. No one was going to keep his money! Frank walked into the Deming National Bank and demanded from the clerk his $1,100. When the clerk refused, Frank presented his withdrawal claim with one hand and drew a Colt .45 with the other. The look he gave the clerk showed he meant business. The clerk unlocked the vault as Frank held a gun on him and handed over the $1,100.

Within hours after the incident, Frank was charged with bank robbery. He was released, but a trial was set. After hearing the charges and examining the evidence, the judge ruled that Frank Thurmond had "acted within his legal rights and could not be charged as the money rightfully belonged to him."

In later years, Frank became the vice-president of the Deming bank that he "robbed" and served in that position until his death.

Lottie outside Kingston with friends. Photo by J. C. Burge, 1880s. J. Marvin Hunter family.

Alfred Henry Lewis (Dan Quin). Photo courtesy of Culver Pictures Inc.

Chapter 12

I t must have been quite a surprise to Frank and Lottie
when they heard from their old friend Dan Quin. Quin,
now using the name Alfred Henry Lewis, wanted to
come out to Deming for a visit. He had known Frank and
Lottie in the days when they were famous as gamblers in
Texas and had told his friends in the East about them and
the many other unusual characters he had come across. His
tales were so interesting that his friends encouraged him to
write them down.

Lewis visited Frank and Lottie in 1896. After his arrival
in Deming, Lewis was taken to their ranch near the Dona
Ana Mountains east of Deming. The three friends sat and
talked about the old days—about Fort Griffin and life on the
Western Trail.

Scholars who have written about Lewis contend that the
town of "Wolfville" in Lewis's series is based on Tombstone,
Arizona. This view is debatable. The geography of Deming
and Silver City matches the locales described in the series
much more closely. In addition, locals in southern New
Mexico feel it is significant that Lewis made extensive notes
while staying with Frank and Lottie and that he began the
series soon after leaving their ranch. There is no question
that Lewis based his characters "Cherokee Hall" on Frank

Thurmond and "Faro Nell" on Lottie. These two characters play major roles in the entire series.

As a writer Lewis had the instincts of a journalist and a preference for writing from real life. He drew on his experiences as a cowboy and on the real-life adventures recollected by friends, including the Thurmonds, rancher Steve Birchfield, and others who had settled in Deming.

William Randolph Hearst agreed to pay a commission for Lewis to publish in his magazines. Hearst was familiar with the Deming area, since his parents, George and Phoebe, had a cattle ranch there. One of Lewis's stories refers to Cow Springs, which was the location of the Hearsts' ranch. In the story "Death in the Don Anas," Lewis places the action in the range of mountains just west of the city of Las Cruces and visible from the ranch owned by the Thurmonds.

In many other Lewis stories, southern New Mexico is the obvious reference point. For example, "The Influence of Faro Nell" refers to Cooke's Peak and the Florida mountain range, both of which are within miles of Deming. The Mexican town in the story is Palomas, which is in Chihuahua, not Sonora, the state directly south of Tombstone.

Deming old-timers familiar with the Wolfville series know that the character in the story called the "Old Cattleman" was none other than the owner of the local Diamond A Ranch, Steve Birchfield. They also know that the town of Red Dog in the stories was Silver City and that the O.K. Restaurant, referred to in another tale, is based on the Broadway, which Lottie Thurmond bought and sold in 1882.

Alfred Henry Lewis recorded, with some exaggeration of their eccentricities, the remarkable western characters he had known. Many of them were southerners who had fought in the Civil War and suffered displacement afterwards. For example, Doc Holliday and Frank Thurmond were both native Georgians, and they were both at Fort Griffin and later in New Mexico, Doc being in Las Vegas in 1879. According to a favorite story told at the Customs House in Deming, Doc Holliday had a drink there. Surely he had good reason to come to New Mexico—to see his old friends.

Herman Lindauer, a member of the family who were closest to the Thurmonds, remembers that "Frank used to read Lewis's *Cosmopolitan* stories as fast as they came off the press and remarked often that they were the only truly authentic stories about the West, Frank's favorite story being the tale about Faro Nell winning back Cherokee's losses to Doc Holliday."

It is told that, during the famous fight with Bailey, Doc Holliday pulled a knife from behind his collar. Frank wore his bowie knife in the same place as Doc, much to Baxter's misfortune on the night he threw the billiard ball at Frank in the saloon. Herman Lindauer stated that "Frank was all Indian; he was faster with a bowie knife than anybody with a gun."

Lewis describes Cherokee Hall in the first book of the Wolfville series:

> "Benev'lent," is the way you puts it! Son, "benev'lent" ain't the word. This Cherokee Hall ain't nothin' short of Char'table.
>
> Speakin' wide flung an' onrestrained, Cherokee, as I mentions to you before, is the modestest, decentest longhorn as ever shakes his antlers in Arizona. He is slim an' light, an' a ondoubted kyard-sharp from his moccasins up.

Mrs. Frank Thurmond, taken in Denison, Texas. Photo by Paul Verden. Courtesy of J. Marvin Hunter family.

Faro Nell is also described:

"Thar's no doubt about it, females is a refinin' an' ennoblin' inflooence; you-all can hazard your chips on that an' pile em higher than Cook's Peak! . . .

"She subdooes the reckless, subjoogates the rebellious, sobers the friv'lous, burns the ground from onder the indolent mocassins of that male she's roped up in holy wedlock's bonds, an' p'ints the way to a higher, happier life."

Home of Lottie and Frank on Pine Street in Deming, New Mexico, as it looked in the 1950s. Courtesy of J. Marvin Hunter family.

Chapter 13

Frank may have been delighted with the Wolfville books, but Lottie did not share his enthusiasm. She found Lewis's characterization of her and Frank offensive. She had never spoken the kind of poor English that Lewis put into the mouth of Faro Nell. She was well educated, and Frank, too, had perfect command of the language.

Lottie was Mrs. Frank Thurmond now, settled in her new and proper life. Her husband was vice-president of the Deming National Bank. He owned a cattle ranch, mines, and real estate. All he ever demanded of her was that she cook his meals, something that people remember Lottie had little interest in doing. She was used to having her meals prepared by servants. She would cook for Frank, but she hated to eat her own cooking, which was doubtless affected by her lack of interest. Therefore, as soon as Frank was gone for the day, Lottie would head out the back door over to the Lindauers for breakfast.

The relationship between Lottie and Helen Lindauer may have been strengthened by the fact that the Lindauers were Jewish. There were very few Jewish families in Deming. Having had her own experiences with anti-Semitism, Lottie may have been especially eager to befriend the Lindauers. Lottie also knew a lot about Judaism and during her

Members of the Lindauer family pictured with Lottie (left). Bertha, Sigmund, and in the front row, Herman, Sam, and Lillian. Lottie spent much of her time with the Lindauers, a Jewish family who were her close friends and near neighbors in Deming. Photo courtesy of Deming Luna Mimbres Museum.

years at the Episcopal girls' school in Kentucky had even learned Hebrew, which was considered appropriate for bible study. She taught a class in Hebrew at the Episcopal church in Deming.

It has been suggested by some who have studied the story of Lottie in Deming that she might have been Jewish herself or her father might have been Jewish or partly Jewish. His business practices, his gambling, and his racing of horses were not characteristic of a well-to-do gentleman with strong Episcopal roots. Sephardic Jews immigrated to America generations earlier and many had intermarried, so this possibility cannot be ruled out, though it would make the family's opposition to Johnny Golden a little harder to account for. Whatever the case, Lottie, despite her strong commitment to the Episcopal church, was familiar with the world of Judaism and acted as a missionary for understanding.

Lottie shared the midday and evening meals with other friends who lived in the same pleasant neighborhood. She often lunched with the Tidmores and had dinner with the Pollards. As Wandra Pollard Smalley recalled in a 1990 interview, "You would know it was Lottie. She would always give her little,'Yoo-Hoo.' Next you would see her smiling face." Wandra Pollard Smalley and Patty Moran Israel, who as children knew Aunt Lottie and Uncle Frank, remembered them very well. Wandra described Lottie as one of her favorite people. Because Lottie had a special way with children—always listening to them and paying special attention to them—she was sometimes called upon to be the sole audience for the productions of the young neighborhood thespians. Wandra and Patty played together as children and would occasionally stage performances in an old

Herman Lindauer as a child. Photo courtesy of Deming Luna Mimbres Museum.

Patty Moran Israel as a child. Photo courtesy of Patty Moran Israel.

carriage house. Lottie would come sit and watch whenever asked, and she also participated in the funeral procession for many a fallen sparrow that the girls would find and provide burial for.

The woman who had watched Smokey Joe and Monte Bill shoot it out, and had lived as a gambler in some of the toughest towns in the West, was now the beloved and favored friend of the children of Deming.

She had not given up her love for cards, and she could always be counted on for a game of bridge. In 1912, twelve wives of Deming's leading businessmen got together to form a unique club, which is still in existence. The group, which called itself the Golden Gossip Club, was at first merely the local sewing circle of the women's club. It grew into more of a social club, with card playing as a central activity. The charter members were Mrs. Steed, Mrs. S. D. Swope, Mrs. C. O. Donaldson, Mrs. W. E. Holt, Mrs. Frank Thurmond, Mrs. J. B. Taylor, Mrs. Bolich, Mrs. Alice Smith, Mrs. J. A. Mahoney, Mrs. John Corbett, Mrs. Shepherd, and Mrs. Pollard. The club, based on a similar organization of the same name in Portage, Wisconsin, had the following motto:

> To tell the best things,
> To make the best of bad things,
> And to straighten mistakes.

Lottie was happy to count as her friends women with a high moral outlook who would accept her as the respectable lady she had always wanted to be.

Lottie's reputation for virtue has been defended by almost all who have written about her and by all in the city of

The Golden Gossip Club founding members. Lottie is pictured in a white dress, seated at the far left. Photo courtesy of Deming Luna Mimbres Museum.

J. Marvin Hunter, author of the book, The Story of Lottie Deno, Her Life and Times. *Photo courtesy of J. Marvin Hunter family.*

Deming who knew her. Patty Moran Israel remembered that Lottie corrected any child whom she caught making a mistake. The children loved her and went to her if they needed help or advice or a smile. She never lost her gaiety or her desire to have a good time. Wandra Pollard Smalley recalled that Lottie always carried her silk dancing shoes in her purse so that she was prepared if any family she was visiting was willing to go out dancing.

In 1993, in a book about Fort Griffin the author quoted information about Lottie's having been fined for operating a house of prostitution there in the Flats. He went further, stating that Lottie had been a prostitute herself. The author was contacted by a friend who said that those remarks had made at least one person in New Mexico very angry. The gentleman who was offended had said that he would be more than happy "to meet the author at high noon to defend the honor of Lottie's character."

J. Marvin Hunter began his 1957 book about Lottie by stating "Lottie Deno was a lady," and his last sentence reads, "She had always been a lady." These statements asserting Lottie's refinement, together with the testimony of all who remember her, make it seem improbable that she was a woman of "low morals," despite the years she lived by gambling. In the Wolfville books, Lewis presents the character Faro Nell as a basically virtuous woman, even in some ways an innocent. Her dedication to Cherokee Hall is a constant throughout the entire series.

Chapter 14

In 1908, Lottie and Frank had been together nearly forty-three years. They knew the West well, were respected for their experience, and were liked by almost everyone (a few of their old enemies might still have held a grudge). Twenty-three of their years together were spent in Deming and the surrounding area. There was never any doubt that this couple cared for each other and always would.

The days grew to a close for them. Frank became ill. The best description of his illness and death is found in the local newspaper, the *Deming Headlight*, in the issues dated June 5 and June 11, 1908. The first reads:

PROMINENT CITIZEN PASSES AWAY
THIS MORNING

Frank Thurmond dies at his residence from cancer of the mouth. [He was] well known throughout the entire west. While not unexpected, the death of Frank Thurmond this morning at 8:15 o'clock has caused a feeling of sadness and regret throughout this entire city. Mr. Thurmond had been sick for several months, although not confined to his bed at all times until the past two months, when he developed cancer in the back part of his mouth and throat. Everything that could be done to relieve him was done, but nothing seemed to avail. Mr. Thurmond, with his now sorrowing wife, had resided in Grant, Sierra, and Luna Counties since the early 80's, and no man in this section was ever more respected. He was the firm friend of every child in any place where he lived and they all went to him in confidence, sure of sympathy. While Mr. Thurmond took a lively interest in all public affairs, and was ever seeking for the upbuilding and advancement of his home town, he steadfastly refused at all times to accept public office of any kind.

Frank Thurmond was born in Atlanta, Ga., in 1840, served with honor in the Confederate army, lived many years in Texas, and was a typical Southern gentleman, which is the best that can be said of any man. The funeral will be held at the family residence at 10:30 o'clock tomorrow.

On June 11, the newspaper published a second account eulogizing Frank and evidently written by a close friend:

FRANK THURMOND

At fifteen minutes after eight o'clock in the forenoon of the 4th of June 1908, Mr. Frank Thurmond died at his residence in Deming, New Mexico. Mr. Thurmond was born in Atlanta, Georgia, on the 21st day of November, in the year 1840. He was never seriously ill prior to the brief illness that terminated in his death, although he had not enjoyed his usual good health since he suffered an attack of la grippe in September of last year. Since that time he had frequently been on trips to the mountains, giving attention to the business of mining, in which he had been interested for many years, and he had frequently appeared on the streets of Deming. He seldom or never talked of himself, and his friends noticed but little, if any, change in him, although at times instead of joining in the general conversation when among his friends as in former years, he seemed not inclined to talk, and appeared to be looking away into the mystic distance—to the end of the way which he was approaching and probably knew by means unknown to those in the vigor of youth and health; but his friends did not know or suspect that his death was so near.

Shortly before his death an abnormal growth appeared in his throat, which was removed by a surgical operation about three weeks before his death. The operation was successful and he recovered from the shock of it, but the growth reappeared within a few days, and it was certain that death must occur within a few weeks or days; and this he fully realized, for about ten days next preceding his death, being conscious almost to the moment of death and able to move around and sit with his good wife under the blooming vines at the home where they lived for so many years. For ten days prior to his death he was fully aware that he was approaching the end of his journey. It was in view. He saw the twilight shadows at the end, and uttered not a word or murmur, but [was] sustained by the calm and unfaltering courage that had characterized all his acts when in the vigor of his life. . . . Mr. Thurmond had no church affiliations and seldom talked upon religious topics, although his ancestors in Georgia were all strong believers in the religion taught by Jesus Christ and members of the church.

Funeral services were conducted by Rev. Sickels of the Presbyterian church, at the home of the deceased. A great many roses and other choice flowers were brought by friends in tender tribute to the departed and laid upon his coffin, so that his lifeless form seemed to be reposing beneath a wilderness of flowers. The tender petals of the flowers must wither and fade; doubtless they have already perished, but their perfume can never be lost. The beautiful words uttered by Rev. Sickles, with the perfume of flowers laid by friends in farewell tribute upon the coffin of the deceased will doubtless live and enter into and cheer the spiritual existence of our departed friend.

As a Georgia boy, Mr. Thurmond entered the Confederate army in 1861 and fought as a private soldier to the end of the war. He accepted the results as a necessity, and said but little about it, but believed as firmly in the justice of the Southern cause up to the day of his death as he did when he joined the Southern army in 1861, and revered the memory of Robert E. Lee, Stonewall Jackson, and other gallant leaders of the Lost Cause. He was a man of deep and abiding convictions, and seldom or never lost confidence in a friend. In person he was tall, slender and wiry, and capable of great endurance. He was emotional and enthusiastic by nature, yet possessed of great self-control and calm in all his physical movements, and ready and willing at all times to lose his life, if necessary, in defense of what he believed to be right. In the presence of men the tenderness and warmth of his real nature was seldom revealed by any physical demonstrations, but at home and among the many little children about town who he loved his unconscious smiles came as sparkles from his heart.

After the war Mr. Thurmond came to Texas, where he

lived for several years, then came with his wife overland to New Mexico, arriving in Silver City July 1, 1880. In 1882, prior to the arrival of the railroad, Mr. Thurmond and his wife came to Deming, where they resided up to the time of Mr. Thurmond's death.

For several years Mr. Thurmond was engaged in the cattle business, and was at all times engaged in the fascinating business of mining, which he pursued with varying fortune, but no matter whether rich or poor he never betrayed a friend and performed all his obligations with scrupulous fidelity, his word being as good as the written bond. At the time of his death, Mr. Thurmond was vice-president of the Deming National Bank, and in comfortable circumstances financially, leaving an estate sufficient to protect his wife from need in all the coming years; but there can be no compensation for a severing of the ties of affection, a parting between friends and loved ones who have been partners for many years, when their lives blended, after they entered upon the sloping way to the grave together with hands joined and hearts united. Mrs. Charlotte Thurmond, surviving wife of the deceased, has the warmest sympathy of many friends in her bereavement. Mr. Thurmond's body was followed to the grave by one of the largest funeral processions ever seen in Deming. In his death Deming loses a true friend and a worthy citizen.

— A Friend.

Chapter 15

L ottie lived on another twenty-six years after Frank's death. Shortly after his death she took a trip to her hometown in Kentucky. It is believed she did not contact any relatives, perhaps out of a lingering fear that she would not be accepted, despite the fact that the face-saving lie concerning a marriage to a wealthy man had in fact come true. It seems that Lottie may never have been able to resolve the loss of old ties to her family and original home.

As a widow Lottie continued to be spunky and outgoing, however. Her love of life was always evident. Although she had no family of her own, her friends in Deming had grown to become a kind of family.

Lottie Deno, the lady gambler, had long since vanished from the scene. Lottie had become Mrs. Frank Thurmond, a longtime resident of the city of Deming. It was only much later, after the development of radio and television, that characters appeared who were based upon the legend of the lady gambler. In the series "Gunsmoke," which was first a radio and then a television show, a beautiful redheaded woman known as Miss Kitty ran a saloon called the Longbranch. The 1957 film *Gunfight at the O.K. Corral*, starring Burt Lancaster, Kirk Douglas, Rhonda Fleming, and Jo Van Fleet, included as characters several historical individuals

Lottie in the early 1900s, about the time J. Marvin Hunter became her friend. Photo courtesy of J. Marvin Hunter family.

*Altar cloth hand crocheted by Mrs. Frank Thurmond for St. Luke's
Episcopal Church and presented on September 22, 1927. Photo courtesy
of Deming Luna Mimbres Museum.*

who had lived at or visited Fort Griffin. Fleming played Laura Denbo, a beautiful redheaded woman gambler with the reputation of being above all else a lady. In the film, Wyatt Earp falls in love with her but then leaves with Doc Holliday to help his brother in Tombstone. When Laura Denbo gets off the stage in Dodge, her luggage consists of a small leather trunk. When Lottie left Fort Griffin, she had a small leather trunk, the one she had bought from Sheriff Jacobs.

In February 1934, Lottie was only a few months away from her ninetieth birthday. She had lived through an unusually difficult time in American history—the period of the Civil War and its aftermath, when so many displaced southerners and northerners found their way west to start anew. She was not to reach ninety. She became ill and was hospitalized, and on February 9, 1934, Lottie died. The *Deming Headlight* reported the following on February 16:

CHARLOTTE THURMOND

Funeral services were held Sunday afternoon at 2:30 for Mrs. Charlotta [sic] Thurmond, beloved pioneer, who died Friday in the Deming Hospital. Until a few days before her death Mrs. Thurmond had maintained her usual good health and cheerful spirit.

Deceased would have been 90 years of age next April. Interment was in Mountainview cemetery, Rev. Wm. Sickel officiating at the grave, as Rev. Ross R. Calvin did at St. Luke's Episcopal Church. Mrs. Thurmond was a native of Kentucky, but had resided in New Mexico since 1878, and in Deming since 1881.

On the same day, February 16, the *Deming Graphic* published this obituary:

CHARLOTTE THURMOND

In the passing of Charlotte Thurmond at the Deming
Hospital Friday, February 9th at noon, Deming lost a
pioneer citizen, whose death is mourned by a host of
friends in New Mexico. Mrs. Thurmond had been in poor
health for only a short time and her illness became critical
a few days before her death.

Mrs. Thurmond was born in Kentucky, and with her
husband, the late Frank Thurmond, arrived in Silver City
by stage in 1878, moving to Deming in 1881, where they
resided ever since, except for one year spent in Kingston,
New Mexico. Mr. Thurmond died in 1908.

She was a member of the Episcopal church, and it was
through her efforts that the church here was built. She
was also a member of the Golden Gossip Club, and never
missed a meeting. She was 89 years old, and had she
lived until April she would have reached her 90th year.
Funeral services were held Sunday at 2:30 p.m. from the
Episcopal church under the direction of G. W. House of
Mahoney's Mortuary, with Rev. R. R. Calvin officiating.
A large attendance filled the chapel and many beautiful
flowers covered the casket as silent tokens of the high
esteem in which Mrs. Thurmond was held by her friends.
Interment was made in the family plot in Mountainview
cemetery, with the following serving as pall bearers: A.
W. Pollard, Herman Lindauer, A. A. Tempke, C. D.
Grabert, and A. W. Marshall. Honorary pall bearers:
Sigmund Lindauer, James Kinnear, J. A. Mahoney, J. A.
Ehrmann, C. J. Kelly, Carl Collins, Dr. Swope, and
Samuel Lindauer. Rev. Sickels spoke at the grave of the
wonderful devoted life, living only to make friends.

*The grave site of Lottie and Frank, Charlotte and Frank Thurmond of
Deming, New Mexico. Frank died at the age of sixty-eight and Lottie at
the age of eighty-nine. Photo by Steve Rose.*

When Lottie's gravestone was set, it was placed a few inches back of the left shoulder of Frank Thurmond. Nell was once again on the lookout chair behind Cherokee. The two now rest together near what was once a towering cottonwood tree in the Odd Fellows section of the Mountainview Cemetery.

* * *

Carlotta J. Thompkins was known by many names during her long life, including the Angel of San Antonio, Mystic Maud, Lottie Deno, and Aunt Lottie, but the name she cherished most was Mrs. Frank Thurmond. Frank was a tough man, adept with a bowie knife. He was a handsome half-breed, part Cherokee, the kind of man that men like Doc Holliday looked up to. Herman Lindauer remembers being on a mining expedition with Frank as a young boy. A mule nearly bit Herman's finger off. He recalls that Uncle Frank gave him a look and a squint of the eye that told the boy to be tough and Herman knew he couldn't cry. It was this man that ended up with the beautiful redheaded Lottie Deno.

Johnny Golden, Lottie's first love, was a victim of the anti-Semitism prevalent after the Civil War. Lottie never forgot the hardships they suffered together, which undoubtedly made her a more tolerant person. Frank Thurmond, as part Cherokee, also knew the ugliness of racism, and Frank was known for his commitment to fairness and equality.

When Frank died, he left Lottie all his possessions. Lottie left her property to Mrs. Allie Bell Stecker (her sister in San Luis Obispo, California), Sigmund Lindauer, and J. A. Mahoney. A few months after Lottie's death, an auction was held at the Thurmond home at 408 Pine Street in Deming. During the auction a small leather trunk was sold to the Reverend J. E. Fuller, the Methodist minister serving in Deming at that time. This was the trunk that, according to popular folklore, "contained some $40,000" when Lottie left Fort Griffin, and it was the trunk that Lottie purchased from Sheriff John C. Jacobs before leaving Texas to join Frank in New Mexico. The trunk was later purchased from Fuller by J. Marvin Hunter, who took it home to Bandera, Texas, where it was later placed in the Frontier Times Museum. The trunk is there today.

The leather trunk purchased by Lottie from Sheriff John C. Jacobs. Photo courtesy of J. Marvin Hunter family.

It still meets today—

The Golden Gossip Club, founded in 1912 by Lottie Deno (Mrs. Frank Thurmond) and eleven other local women, has survived two world wars and the Great Depression and continues to meet every week in Deming, New Mexico, for card-playing and the celebration of lasting frienship.

Fred Harvey Lunchroom, Deming, New Mexico, 1901. Photo courtesy Museum of New Mexico (Negative no. 66011).

The town of Deming came out to greet President William McKinley at the railroad depot, May 6, 1901. Photo by Thomas Risdon; courtesy Museum of New Mexico (Negative no. 56298).